Cat Club

American Shorthairs

by Cameron L. Woodson

Ideas for Parents and Teachers

Bullfrog Books let children practice reading informational text at the earliest reading levels. Repetition, familiar words, and photo labels support early readers.

Before Reading
- Discuss the cover photo. What does it tell them?
- Look at the picture glossary together. Read and discuss the words.

Read the Book
- "Walk" through the book and look at the photos. Let the child ask questions. Point out the photo labels.
- Read the book to the child, or have him or her read independently.

After Reading
- Prompt the child to think more. Ask: American shorthairs love to play! Can you think of other kinds of pets that like to play?

Bullfrog Books are published by Jump!
5357 Penn Avenue South
Minneapolis, MN 55419
www.jumplibrary.com

Library of Congress Cataloging-in-Publication Data

Names: Woodson, Cameron L., 1994– author.
Title: American shorthairs / Cameron L. Woodson.
Description: Minneapolis: Jump!, Inc., [2021]
Series: Cat club | Includes index.
Audience: Ages 5–8 | Audience: Grades K–1
Identifiers: LCCN 2019048801 (print)
LCCN 2019048802 (ebook)
ISBN 9781645274452 (hardcover)
ISBN 9781645274469 (ebook)
Subjects: LCSH: American shorthair cat
Juvenile literature.
Classification: LCC SF449.A45 W66 2021 (print)
LCC SF449.A45 (ebook)
DDC 636.8/2—dc23
LC record available at https://lccn.loc.gov/2019048801
LC ebook record available at
https://lccn.loc.gov/2019048802

Editors: Jenna Gleisner and Susanne Bushman
Designer: Jenna Casura

Photo Credits: Paisit Teeraphatsakool/Shutterstock, cover, 1; alexavol/Shutterstock, 3, 8l, 9 (foreground), 23br, 24; Linn Currie/Shutterstock, 4; Cat'chy Images/Shutterstock, 5, 8m, 8r; Olga Nikanovich/Shutterstock, 6–7 (cat); Bebenjy/iStock, 6–7 (hand); Sasin Paraksa/Shutterstock, 9 (background), 23br; Somphop Krittayaworagul/Shutterstock, 10–11; gerard lacz/Alamy, 12–13; ANURAK PONGPATIMET/Shutterstock, 14–15, 20–21, 23tl, 23tr; Eric Isselee/Shutterstock, 16; nikniknik/Shutterstock, 17; Silarock/Shutterstock, 18–19, 23bl; photo by Volchanskiy/iStock, 22.

Printed in the United States of America at Corporate Graphics in North Mankato, Minnesota.

Table of Contents

Popular Pets

This is an American shorthair!

Its fur is short.
That is why
we call it a
shorthair!

5

brush

These cats are popular pets.

Why?

They are easy to care for.

They can be many colors.

Many are
silver tabby.

silver
tabby

9

Their eyes can be many colors, too.

Like what?

This one has green eyes!

Cool!

These cats are fast.
Their legs are strong.
They can jump high.

See this kitten pounce?
Cute!

kitten

15

These cats have sharp claws. They can use them to hunt!

claw

These cats are fun.
They love to play!

toy

17

They like to be petted.

They purr.

Would you like an American shorthair?

An American Shorthair Up Close

An American shorthair has strong, muscular legs and large eyes. Its fur is short. Look at its other body parts!

tail

ear

eye

nose

whiskers

fur

paw

Picture Glossary

popular
Liked by many people.

pounce
To jump forward and grab
something suddenly.

purr
To make a low, vibrating
sound in the throat.

tabby
Striped with a darker color.

Index

To Learn More

FACT SURFER

Finding more information is as easy as 1, 2, 3.

❶ Go to www.factsurfer.com

❷ Enter "Americanshorthairs" into the search box.

❸ Click the "Surf" button to see a list of websites.